Lulu and Lainey

... 12 Days of Christmas

by Lois Petren

illustrated by Tanja Russita

Other books by Lois Petren:

Lulu and Lainey … a French Yarn
Lulu and Lainey … a Christmas Yarn
Lulu and Lainey … the Lucky Day
Lulu and Lainey … at the Farm
Lulu and Lainey … Color with Us
Five Enchanted Mermaids Coloring and Activity Book

To grandmothers, everywhere.

Copyright © 2018 Lois Petren

All rights reserved.

Paperback ISBN-13: 978-1-720268420
Hardcover ISBN-13: 978-0-9998099-5-2

Lulu loved to knit with her Grand-mère. She especially loved to knit gifts for family and friends for Christmas.

Of course she always had her favorite ball of yarn – the one she called Lainey – in her knitting basket!

All through the year they worked together on projects so they would be ready to surprise everyone at Christmas.

It made Lulu so happy and proud to see the smiles on their faces when they opened their presents. It was almost better than getting gifts!

One day Lulu and Grand-mère were baking holiday cookies. They sang carols together and happily chatted about all the presents they had made and who would receive them.

Suddenly, Lulu exclaimed: "Grand-mère, it's just like the carol about the 12 Days of Christmas! I have an idea. Let's make up our own song about it!"

And, that's exactly what they did.

On the first day of Christmas, Lulu gave to cousin Nicole a baby blanket shaped like a star.

On the second day of Christmas, Lulu gave to Maman two lacy shawls.

On the third day of Christmas, Lulu gave to cousin Paul three stylish sweaters.

On the fourth day of Christmas, Lulu gave to Papa four knitted scarves.

On the fifth day of Christmas, Lulu gave to Tante Eloise five shopping sacks.

On the sixth day of Christmas, Lulu gave to Noémi six dancing dolls.

On the seventh day of Christmas, Lulu gave to Oncle Jacque seven dapper vests.

On the eighth day of Christmas, Lulu gave to Grand-mère eight dainty tea cozies.

On the ninth day of Christmas, Lulu gave to her neighbors' pets nine doggie sweaters.

On the tenth day of Christmas, Lulu gave to Bertie ten fuzzy mittens.

On the eleventh day of Christmas, Lulu gave to Pierre eleven cozy hats.

On the twelfth day of Christmas, Lulu gave to Grand-père twelve woolly socks.

They enjoyed their new song so much that they sang it again and again. Finally, all the cookies were baked and decorated.

Then Grand-mère said, "It's time to wrap our gifts so we can deliver them."

The next day Lulu and Grand-mère went out with the gifts. Lulu said, "This is more fun than receiving presents, except for the ones that Père Noël leaves for me. Now I know why he is so cheerful!"

Grand-mère smiled and replied, "Yes, giving presents is one of the happiest things we can do."

They wished everyone Joyeux Noël and headed home – very happy, indeed. As they arrived home they sang their carol one last time:

"On the twelfth day of Christmas Lulu gave lots of gifts:

twelve woolly socks,
eleven cozy hats,
ten fuzzy mittens,
nine doggie sweaters,
eight dainty tea cozies,
seven dapper vests,
six dancing dolls,
five shopping sacks,
four knitted scarves,
three stylish sweaters,
two lacy shawls,
and a baby blanket shaped like a star!"

I hope you enjoyed this book.

Be sure to visit www.loisapetren.com to learn more about the world of Lulu and Lainey.

Made in the USA
San Bernardino, CA
18 November 2018